Where's the water?

EARTH'S OCEANS

By Peter Castellano

Gareth Stevens
PUBLISHING

Please visit our website, www.garethstevens.com. For a free color catalog of all our high-quality books, call toll free 1-800-542-2595 or fax 1-877-542-2596.

Library of Congress Cataloging-in-Publication Data

Names: Castellano, Peter, author.
Title: Earth's oceans / Peter Castellano.
Description: New York : Gareth Stevens Pub., 2017. | Series: Where's the water? | Includes index.
Identifiers: LCCN 2016000751 | ISBN 9781482446791 (pbk.) | ISBN 9781482446784 (library bound) | ISBN 9781482446760 (6 pack)
Subjects: LCSH: Ocean–Juvenile literature.
Classification: LCC GC21.5 .C38 2017 | DDC 551.46–dc23
LC record available at http://lccn.loc.gov/2016000751

First Edition

Published in 2017 by
Gareth Stevens Publishing
111 East 14th Street, Suite 349
New York, NY 10003

Copyright © 2017 Gareth Stevens Publishing

Designer: Katelyn E. Reynolds
Editor: Kristen Nelson

Photo credits: Cover, p. 1 artcasta/Shutterstock.com; cover, pp. 1–24 (background) vitalez/Shutterstock.com; pp. 4–21 (circle splash) StudioSmart/Shutterstock.com; p. 5 Alexander Gerst/ESA via Getty Images; p. 7 aragami12345s/Shutterstock.com; pp. 9, 11, 13 (map) Intrepix/Shutterstock.com; p. 9 (inset) The Asahi Shimbun via Getty Images; p. 11 (main) Oskari Porkka/Shutterstock.com; p. 15 (main) Volt Collection/Shutterstock.com; pp. 15, 17 (map) ugljesa/Shutterstock.com; p. 17 (main) Tsuguliev/Shutterstock.com; p. 19 Frolova_Elena/Shutterstock.com.

Printed in the United States of America

CPSIA compliance information: Batch #CS16GS : For further information contact Gareth Stevens, New York, New York at 1-800-542-2595.

CONTENTS

Words in the glossary appear in **bold** type the first time they are used in the text.

ONE WORLD OCEAN

If you looked at Earth from space, you'd see there's only one ocean. It's a body of salt water that covers more than 70 percent of our planet! But **geologists**, map makers, and world leaders have set **boundaries** to separate this large body so that it's easier to talk about where things are on Earth. The seven **continents** are often part of the boundaries.

Today, there are five named oceans: the Pacific, the Atlantic, the Indian, the Southern, and the Arctic Oceans.

From space, you'd never be able to tell where one named ocean ends and another begins!

CONSTANT CHANGES

The oceans' water is contained in very large basins, or dips in Earth's surface shaped somewhat like bowls. The basins have changed a lot over time as the large plates that make up Earth's **crust** have moved. The movement of these plates has created deep **trenches**.

As plates smash into one another, they form ridges, which look like huge underwater mountain chains. Lava may flow out of cracks in the crust, too. When it cools, it makes new rock, changing the ridges even more!

Facts on Tap

The Mid-Atlantic Ridge formed where the two plates that make up the floor of the Atlantic ocean meet. It's about 10,000 miles (16,100 km) long!

Underwater ridges sometimes reach the ocean's surface as islands. The Azores Islands in Portugal, pictured here, are the highest points of the Mid-Atlantic Ridge.

THE PEACEFUL PACIFIC

Explorer Ferdinand Magellan sailed into what's now called the Pacific Ocean in the early 1500s. He was the first person to call it "pacific," which comes from a Latin word meaning "peaceful."

The Pacific Ocean is the largest named ocean, covering more of Earth than all the land put together. It touches Asia, Australia, North America, and South America. The Pacific is also the deepest ocean, including the deepest spot on Earth, Challenger Deep, which is more than 36,000 feet (10,970 m) deep.

Facts on Tap

The Pacific Ocean stretches from the Arctic to the Antarctic areas on Earth. This makes it hard to call out special features of the ocean since it's part of so many different climates.

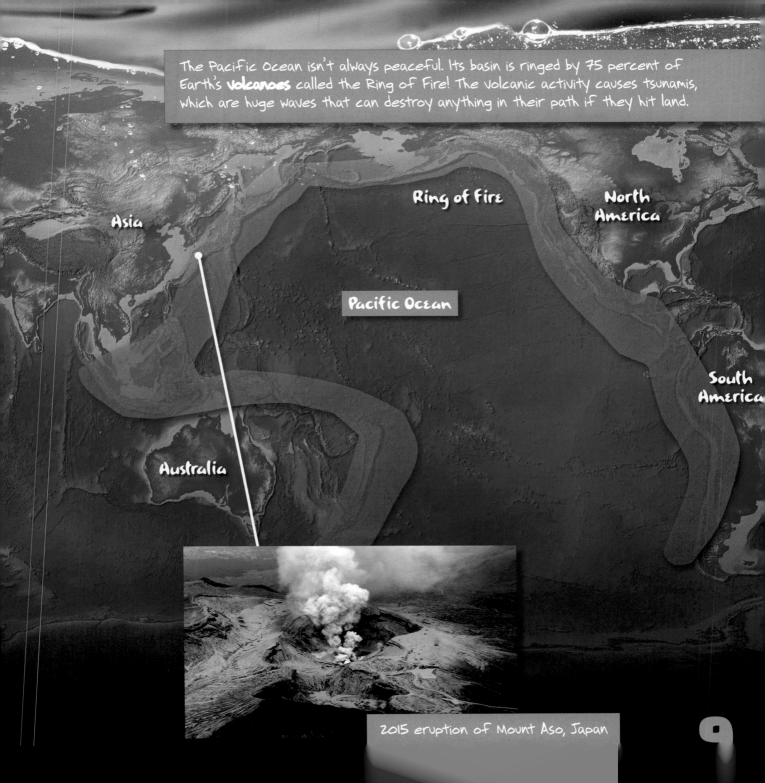

The Pacific Ocean isn't always peaceful. Its basin is ringed by 75 percent of Earth's **volcanoes** called the Ring of Fire! The volcanic activity causes tsunamis, which are huge waves that can destroy anything in their path if they hit land.

Asia

Ring of Fire

North America

Pacific Ocean

South America

Australia

2015 eruption of Mount Aso, Japan

9

THE MIGHTY ATLANTIC

The second-largest ocean is the Atlantic Ocean, covering about 20 percent of Earth's surface. It has North America and South America as its western boundary and Europe and Africa as its eastern boundary. Though all oceans on Earth are salt water, the Atlantic is the saltiest!

The line of **latitude** that divides Earth, the equator, is used to separate the Atlantic Ocean into the North Atlantic and South Atlantic. The Mid-Atlantic Ridge also runs through the Atlantic north to south, creating two main basins.

Facts on Tap

The northern boundary of the Atlantic Ocean is often set at the Arctic Circle, which is a line of latitude that contains the northernmost part of Earth.

The Atlantic Ocean formed about 180 million years ago when the landmasses on Earth began to break apart and move to their present places.

North America

Europe

North Atlantic

Africa

South America

South Atlantic

THE INDIAN OCEAN

About one-fifth of the water covering Earth is part of the Indian Ocean. The bounds of the Indian Ocean are the eastern coast of Africa, the west coasts of Indonesia and Australia, and the southern coast of India.

What's the southern limit of the Indian Ocean? It depends on whom you ask. Some say it reaches the coast of Antarctica. But many people, especially from Australia, say that area of water is part of the Southern Ocean.

Facts on Tap

The Indian Ocean is the third-largest ocean on Earth.

The Indian Ocean touches the Atlantic Ocean around the southern tip of Africa and meets the Pacific Ocean to the east of Australia and Asia.

India

Africa

Indonesia

Indian Ocean

Australia

A "NEW" OCEAN?

In 2000, many scientists decided to give the ocean around Antarctica its own name—the Southern Ocean, or the Antarctic Ocean. They took away the southernmost parts of the Atlantic, the Indian, and the Pacific Oceans to create this "new" ocean.

The Southern Ocean's northernmost boundary has yet to be set, but will likely be either 60°S or 50°S latitude. Its surface will be about twice the size of the United States, making it the fourth-largest ocean on Earth.

Facts on Tap

The Southern Ocean's **temperature** is commonly between 28°F and 50°F (-2°C and 10°C). You wouldn't want to swim in that!

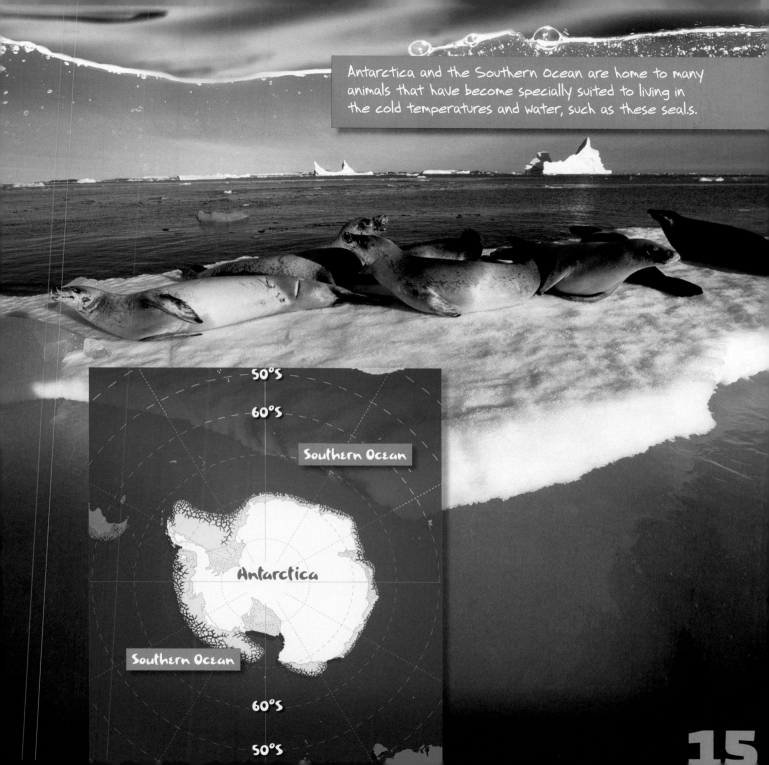

Antarctica and the Southern Ocean are home to many animals that have become specially suited to living in the cold temperatures and water, such as these seals.

50°S

60°S

Southern Ocean

Antarctica

Southern Ocean

60°S

50°S

TO THE NORTH

The center of the Arctic Ocean is the North Pole! It's no wonder that the Arctic Ocean is the coldest ocean on Earth. It's so far north, it's almost always covered with ice nearly 10 feet (3 m) thick on average.

The Arctic Ocean is also the smallest and shallowest ocean on Earth. It's only about one-sixth the size of the Indian Ocean and the deepest point that's been recorded is only about 18,050 feet (5,500 m) deep.

Facts on Tap

The Arctic Ocean is almost completely surrounded by land, including North America, Greenland, Europe, and Asia.

Not many people have traveled the Arctic Ocean because of its thick ice. Ships can get stuck in it!

North America

Arctic Ocean

Asia

North Pole

Greenland

Europe

SEAS

Seas are smaller than oceans and are most often places where the ocean meets land or where land encloses ocean water. There are inland seas, too, such as the Caspian Sea.

Two of the biggest seas on Earth are connected to the Atlantic Ocean. The Mediterranean Sea is found between Europe and Africa, with the Atlantic Ocean to the west and Asia to the east. The Caribbean Sea has Central America to its west and South America to its south.

facts on Tap

All seas contain salt water, even those inland.

The Caribbean Sea is tropical, which means it's found near the equator where it's hot. Its water is commonly around 80°F (27°C).

19

CARING FOR EARTH'S OCEANS

The people who live on Earth have a great effect on the health of the oceans. Pollution, such as the burning of **fossil fuels**, has caused Earth to slowly grow warmer. This is called global climate change. Over time, rising temperatures cause the ice to melt, increasing ocean levels. This harms the animals and plants that live in the ocean.

Groups around the world help clean up pollution along coastlines and work to reduce fossil fuel use. You can join them to keep our oceans healthy!

Facts on Tap

Scientists have found that the amount of ice covering the Arctic Ocean shrinks about 8 percent every 10 years. This is because of the rising temperatures on Earth.

Earth's Oceans

	surface area (excluding seas)	average depth	deepest point
Pacific Ocean	63.8 million square miles (165.24 million sq km)	14,040 feet (4,280 m)	36,201 feet (11,034 m)
Atlantic Ocean	31.8 million square miles (82.36 million sq km)	10,925 feet (3,300 m)	27,493 feet (8,380 m)
Indian Ocean	28.4 million square miles (73.5 million sq km)	12,990 feet (3,960 m)	24,442 feet (7,450 m)
Southern Ocean	7.8 million square miles (20.2 million sq km)*	13,000 to 16,000 feet (3,962 to 4,877 m)	23,736 feet (7,235 m)
Arctic Ocean	5.4 million square miles (13.9 million sq km)	3,240 feet (988 m)	18,050 feet (5,500 m)

GLOSSARY

boundary: a place that marks the limit of something

climate: the average weather conditions of a place over a period of time

continent: one of Earth's seven great landmasses

crust: the outer shell of a planet

fossil fuel: matter formed over millions of years from plant and animal remains that is burned for power

geologist: someone who studies geology, or the science that studies the history of Earth and its life as recorded in rocks

latitude: the imaginary lines that run east and west above and below the equator

stretch: to reach across

temperature: how hot or cold something is

trench: a long, narrow cut in the ground

volcano: an opening in a planet's surface through which hot,

FOR MORE INFORMATION

Books

Oachs, Emily Rose. *Southern Ocean*. Minneapolis, MN: Bellwether Media, Inc., 2016.

Roumanis, Alexis. *Oceans*. New York, NY: AV2, 2016.

World Book. *Oceans and Climate Change*. Chicago, IL: World Book, 2016.

Websites

Ocean Facts!
ngkids.co.uk/science-and-nature/Ocean-Facts
Find out National Geographic Kids' top 10 ocean facts!

Oceans for Kids
ducksters.com/geography/oceans.php
Read more about Earth's oceans here.

INDEX

EPIC
ADVENTURES
PUZZLE
BOOK

Dover Publications, Inc.
Mineola, New York

This Dover edition, first published in 2018,
is an unabridged republication of the work originally
published by Arcturus Publishing Limited, London.

ISBN-13: 978-0-486-82851-0
ISBN-10: 0-486-82851-4

82851401   2018
www.doverpublications.com

Written by Dr. Gareth Moore
Illustrated by Moreno Chiacchiera, with Martyn Cain
Cover illustration by Giorgia Broseghini
Designed by oakleycreative.co.uk

Manufactured in China by 1010 Printing International Ltd.

Contents

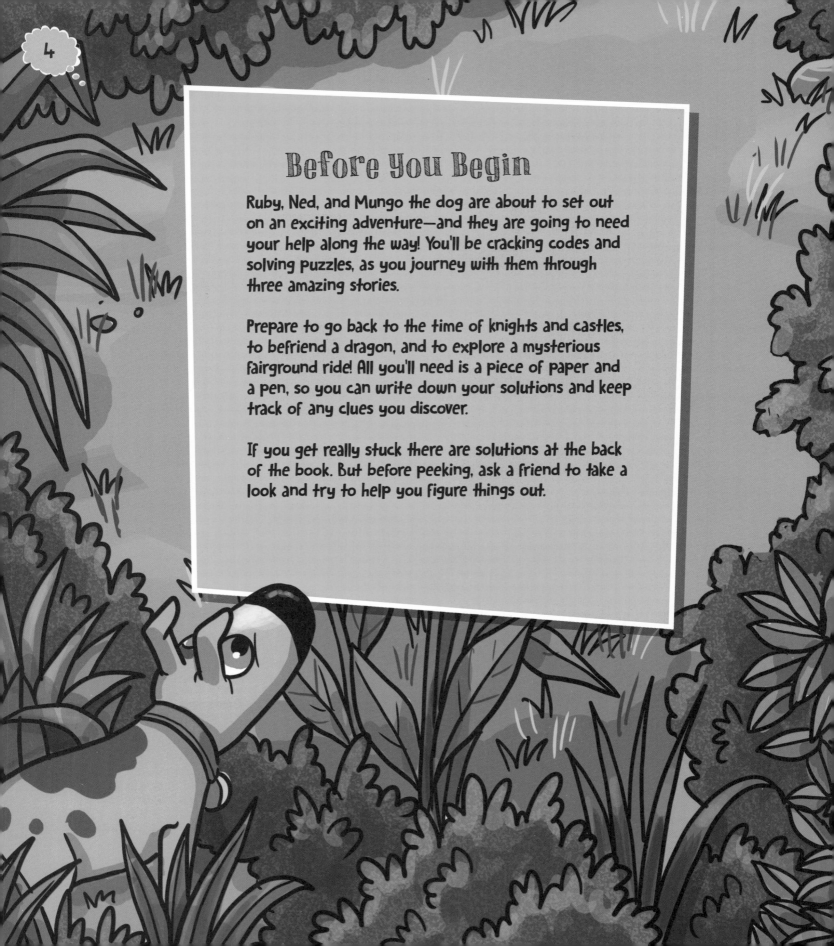

Before You Begin

Ruby, Ned, and Mungo the dog are about to set out on an exciting adventure—and they are going to need your help along the way! You'll be cracking codes and solving puzzles, as you journey with them through three amazing stories.

Prepare to go back to the time of knights and castles, to befriend a dragon, and to explore a mysterious fairground ride! All you'll need is a piece of paper and a pen, so you can write down your solutions and keep track of any clues you discover.

If you get really stuck there are solutions at the back of the book. But before peeking, ask a friend to take a look and try to help you figure things out.

The Magic Castle

Ruby, her best friend Ned, and her dog Mungo are visiting the ruins of an ancient castle. Mungo, who is leading the way, runs ahead. Will you join the three of them as they explore the castle and help discover its surprising secrets?

Roundabout Writing

Ruby pulls at the boards over the fireplace, and they come loose. Hidden behind is a concealed corridor, leading to a room with a strange machine in the middle. This machine doesn't look medieval! What can it be for? Ruby hopes it is not dangerous, as Mungo seems to have climbed inside it and gotten stuck. Perhaps finding the missing cogs will free Mungo. Can you work out where they are?

Spied a Spider?

Ruby and Ned spot the trapdoor that hides the missing cogs. They want to open it, but there is a bug on top. Is it safe to open? Neds knows that the black creeper spider is very dangerous, but the similar-looking black creeper insect is harmless. Which is it?

Under the Floor

Aha! The missing cogs! Ruby finds a note, too. She reads it out loud. "To ★ make + the ★ machine + work, ★ you + need ★ only + two ★ cogs." But which ones? Can you find them?

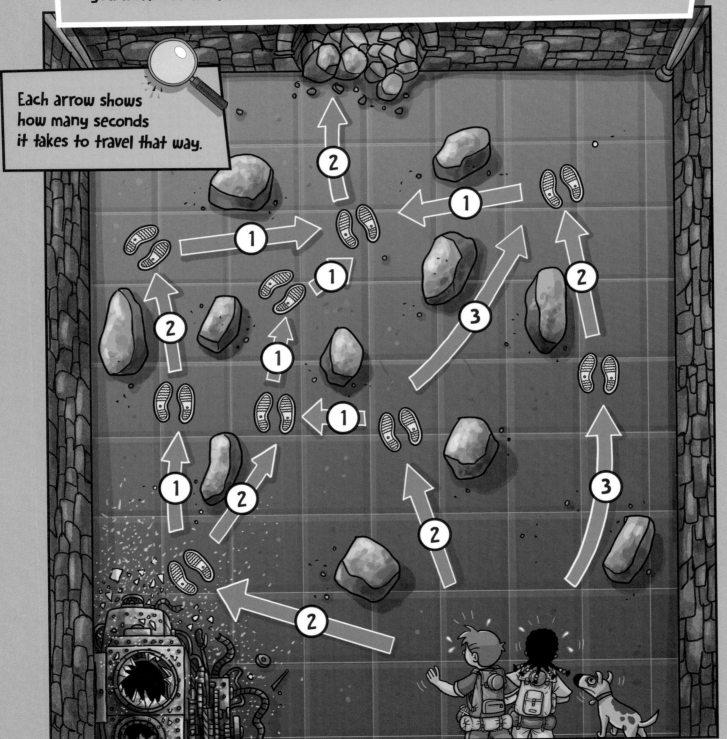

Flee the Room

After Ned's shout, the rocks stop falling. The doorway has been partly blocked, but there is a small gap for the kids to squeeze through. A countdown begins! Can you work out the fastest route to leave this room, before anything else happens?

Each arrow shows how many seconds it takes to travel that way.

The Magic Castle

Ruby looks out of the window and is astonished by what she sees. They are very high up, and the view is slowly moving. "The castle is flying!" Luckily, Ruby spots something that may give them a clue as to what is going on. Can you find it, too?

Coded Message

Tucked beneath the window sill, Ruby finds a folded piece of paper. They open it and discover a secret code! Some of the letters have been translated into English, but not all of them. Can you work out what the missing words say by comparing the matching symbols?

The Knights' Watch

The message seems useless, but Ruby puts the paper in her pocket anyway. Ruby, Ned, and Mungo continue through the castle. In the next room are some mechanical knights, holding fearsome-looking weapons. The children decide it is best to avoid them! Can you find a safe route through the room, without making them start moving?

Due to their helmets, these knights can only see the tiles in a straight line in front of them. Their view is blocked by bookcases.

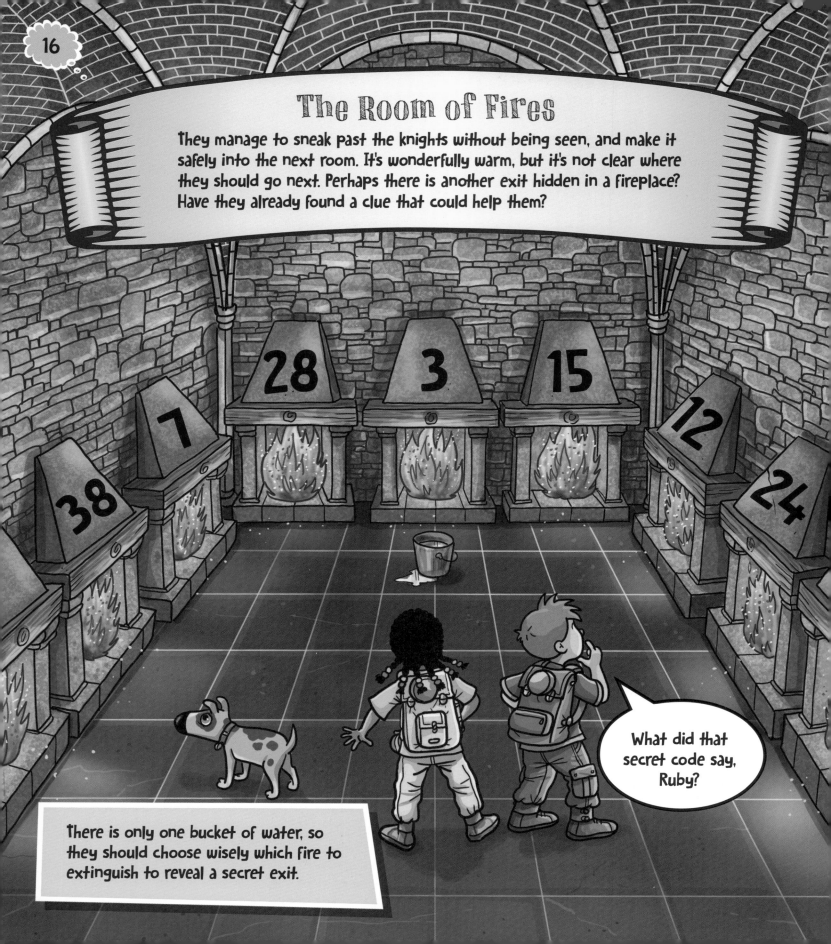

Inside the Castle Walls

Ned, Ruby, and Mungo crawl carefully through the fireplace. The floor is still a little hot! They find themselves in a narrow corridor, which they soon discover is part of a maze of secret passages hidden within the castle walls! Can you help them find their way to the door?

The children can go up and down the ladders, and jump over the gaps in the floor. However, once they drop through a trapdoor, they can't go back!

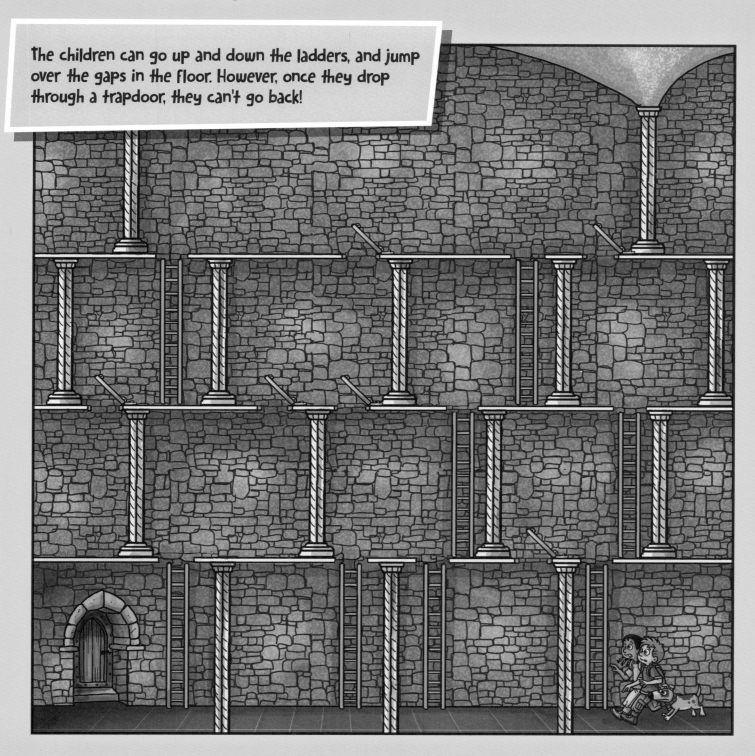

Skeleton Key

Made it! Ruby, Ned, and Mungo emerge from the maze of passages into a dusty room, which was probably once the castle dungeon. Ned soon finds out that the door out of this room is locked. One of the skeletons is holding the correct key, but can you work out which one?

Riddle me this. Who is in charge of this castle? They have a woman to their left, blue eyes, and they are right-handed.

Food!

a Medieval Feast

They unlock the door and step into what appears to be a medieval hall. A feast is in full swing! A server approaches them. "Please, can you help us find our way out of this castle?" asks Ned. "Of course," replies the server, whose name is Jack. "But first you must solve my riddle!"

The Kitchen Door

Jack tells them to meet him in the kitchen. Which of these doors should they go through? There might be a clue if you remember what he was wearing.

The Kitchen

Jack has to finish his tasks before he can show the children which way to go. Can you help him?

The Missing Silverware

Poor Jack! He was just about to take Ned and Ruby to the secret passageway, but he has been given two more urgent jobs to do first. Ned and Ruby do their best to help him. the first task is to find some silverware.

Juicy bones!

Can you help me to find knives, forks, and spoons? I need two of each!

Quick on the Drawer

Finally, Jack has to work out how the silverware should be placed in the drawer.

I know that the knives go in a slot to the left of the forks, and that the spoons are placed in neither the leftmost nor the rightmost slot. Where should they all go? Can you show me?

The Secret Panel

At last, Jack's tasks are complete! Now he can finally help Ruby, Ned, and Mungo find their way out of the castle. Jack tells them that one of the paintings on this wall is a secret panel. It will open if tapped in the right way—but where is it hidden?

The Knights' Revenge

The door opens onto a large room where mechanical knights are standing guard. "Not again!" groans Ned. Jack has to get back to his chores. But before he goes, he warns, "Only step on the six-sided stones." Can you find a route to the other side, without waking the knights?

The Control Room

Well now, this is not something you expect in a medieval castle! However, this is a rather strange castle, after all. This control panel will help Ruby and Ned get back home, if only they can figure out how it works.

Using the controls in this room, you can command the castle to fly *wherever* you wish. But first, you must enter the right code.

Look carefully across each row and down each column. Then decide the order to press each button on the panel below!

Park the Castle

Ruby and Ned program the destination into the computer. A screen lights up on the control panel, as the castle makes its final calculations for returning home. Each line contains a number sequence, but each one is missing a vital number. Can you work out the correct values to enter into the computer?

2	4	6	8	_____
4	7	10	13	_____
27	22	17	12	_____
2	4	8	16	_____
45	41	37	33	_____

The first one must be 10, because each number is 2 larger than the previous one.

The first one is easy! Can you do the rest?

Leaving the Castle

The castle has landed safely, and is back to its old, ruined appearance. Ruby, Ned, and Mungo need to get back down to the ground. The computer says, "Only use the ladders with an odd number of rungs." How do they do it?

Down from the Walls

They are almost at the bottom, but wait! Not everything has gone back to normal. There are still some mechanical knights nearby. Some are even camouflaged! How many are there? If Ned and Ruby can find them all, they can creep past!

Goodbye!

Ruby, Ned, and Mungo creep past all of the knights and make it safely out of the castle. When they are a safe distance away, they turn around to look. The ruins are exactly as they found them at the start of their adventure, and all traces of the medieval occupants are now gone—or are they? Can you spot what Ruby and Ned have seen?

The Mysterious Woods

Ned, Ruby, and her dog Mungo are out for a walk in the woods. They are busy admiring the pretty flowers when all of a sudden they hear a loud sneeze, and see sparks shooting into the sky like fireworks.

Muddy Clues

The children spot an information board showing them how to recognize an animal from its footprint. There are certainly plenty of footprints in the mud here. Can you see which animals have been here? What has Mungo spotted?

Follow the Trail

Ned, Ruby, and Mungo find a path behind the bush. It branches into several different routes. "Look," says Ruby. "Weird patches of burned grass! Let's search them all for clues."

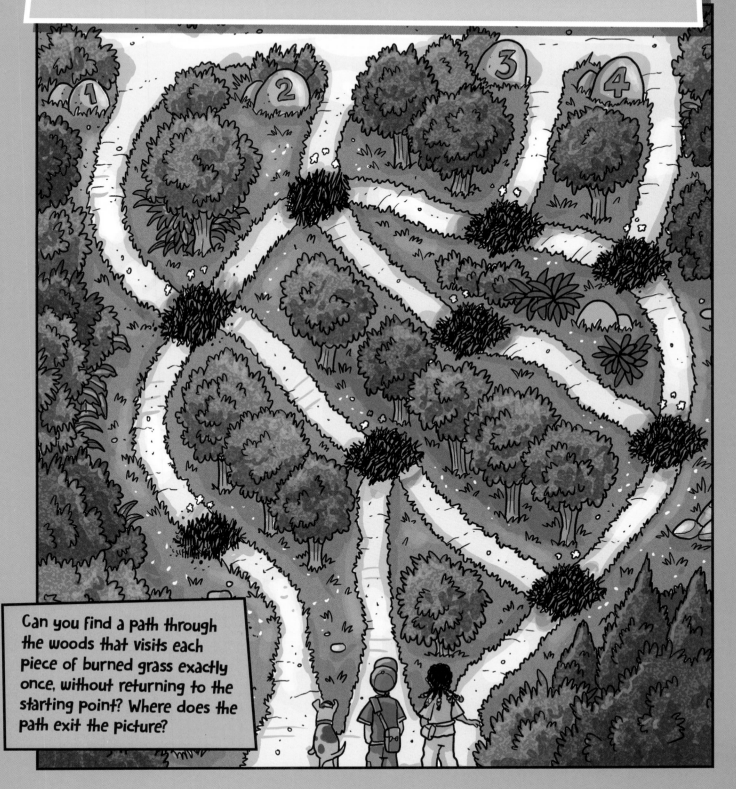

Can you find a path through the woods that visits each piece of burned grass exactly once, without returning to the starting point? Where does the path exit the picture?

The Mysterious Map

Ned discovers a notebook in one of the patches of burned grass. They walk a little farther, and Ned gives a shout. "Look! There's a map of this clearing in the notebook!" There are instructions, too. "Start at the bee. North 6, West 2, South 4, East 8, South 2, West 2." Where do the kids end up?

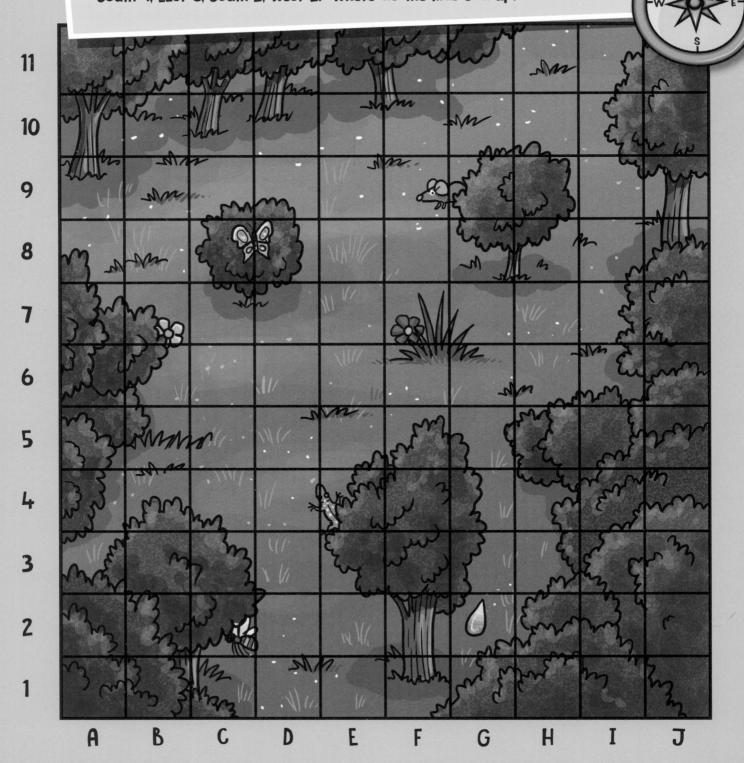

Look in the Book

They find a pink scale lying in the grass. Ned picks it up. "I think the scale wants us to go this way," he says, surprised. "Wait!" says Ruby, "We need to know what creature we're dealing with. I think there might be a clue in the notebook."

Taking Flight

It IS a dragon, and he seems to be in trouble. Can you understand his magic language?

⊛ HEAVY
● ARE
✷ HAVE
♎ THE
☠ ACCIDENT
◆ TRAPPED
◉ FLOWERS
❖ LOVELY
■ MAGICALLY

"Whenever I sneeze, I cast a spell!" says the dragon. "My last sneeze must have made these flowers heavy." In what order should you take them away to free him?

Muddled Story

"My name is Snuffles," says the dragon. He starts explaining how he became trapped, but he sneezes again, and his words are magically rearranged. Can you understand him?

Mysterious Changes

Snuffles the dragon seems very taken with Ned's hat. As the children talk to him, he sneezes again. There is a flash of light, and suddenly the hat is on the dragon's head!

There are five other differences, too. Can you see them?

Sleeping Dragons

Ned and Ruby come to a room that is full of sleepy dragons. They tiptoe past very quietly, so as not to disturb them. They need to find the treasure room quickly to get Ned's hat back!

What have Ned and Ruby missed?

Into the Garden

Snuffles then asks Ruby and Ned if they want to see the most valuable treasure of all. The children say yes, and the dragon leads them out ... into a garden full of flowers! He is a garden dragon, after all.

Ruby and Ned love the shape of the flowerbeds. Can you work out which of the garden maps matches the garden they can see?

Mungo Finds Some Flowers

Mungo wanders over to some huge flowers. Snuffles gets excited. "Let's pick some as a gift for my parents," he says. Snuffles wants to pick as many as possible, but he wants to make sure his bunch of flowers has an even number of petals in total. What is the maximum number of flowers he can give them?

Which Watering Can?

Snuffles's parents love the flowers he picked for them, and can't wait to plant some more. However, Snuffles's dad has lost his magical watering can, which helps the flowers to grow extra large! Can you help him to find it?

a Handful of Jewels!

The dragons are very happy with the help the children have given them. Snuffles's dad holds out a paw with some precious jewels in it. He asks Ned to pick one and to make sure he chooses the one with a different number of sides from all the others.

Gem-tastic

Now it is Ruby's turn. She picks the jewel that was not shown to Ned. Can you work out which one it is?

Trading Gifts

It's time to go. Ned gives his hat to Snuffles. "Perhaps it will help with all the sneezing." In exchange, the dragon gives them something from the treasure room: an object that all of the treasure chests contained. What is it? See page 46 for clues.

Looking Down

Ned and Ruby have a great view of the countryside from the back of the dragon. They just have to decide where to land.

CLUE:
What is Ned holding?

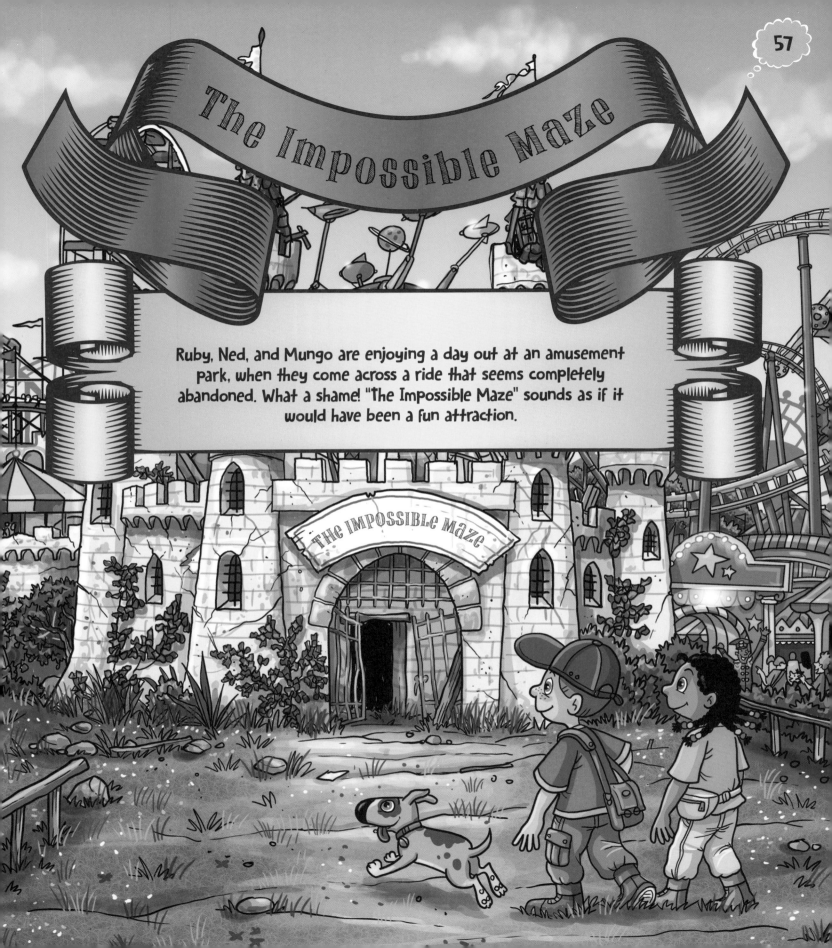

Roller Coasters

Ruby and Ned want to investigate, but they don't want to use the front door! They decide to look for another way in. There are three roller coasters nearby, which might help. Which one should they ride to get a better view of the Impossible Maze?

a Closer Look

The roller coaster travels around and around the theme park until it passes by the roof of the Impossible Maze. Can you spot a way for them to get into the building via the roof?

The Trapdoor

Ruby and Ned reach the roof and find the trapdoor they saw from the roller coaster. It is locked with a padlock, though. Can you find a hidden key that they can use to open it?

Message Board

Ruby spots a sign that might have useful information on it. Can you work out what it says?

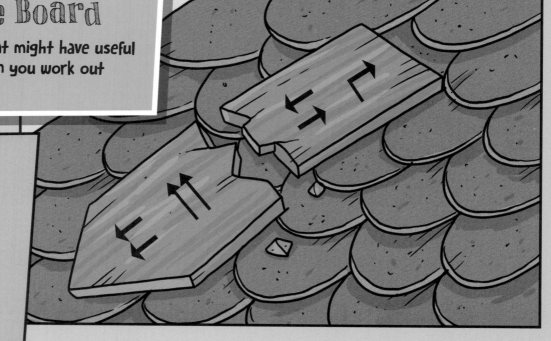

↺ ENEMIES
↰ OPEN
⇇ THE
⇈ GOBLINS
↶ RIDE
↱ FRIENDLY
↪ UNICORNS
↴ ARE
↻ IS

another Lock

Luckily, Ruby spots another key, and this one works. She opens the padlock, but instead of releasing the trapdoor, the lock springs open to reveal three number dials, plus a sheet of instructions that they unfold and read. What is the three-digit code they need to open the padlock?

to open the padlock, add the number of days in a leap year to the number of keys on the keyring.

Mirror Mirror

The goblin—whose name is Garibaldi—nods as the children pick the correct maze. He tells them he needs to give them one more test before they can continue, then he suddenly darts off. The children follow Garibaldi, only to discover him standing in front of some mirrors.

Children, can you solve this puzzle, too? Which mirror shows my form most true?

Which of the magical reflections exactly matches Garibaldi?

The Goblin's Tale

Garibaldi tells Ned and Ruby his tale. The Impossible Maze was once the most wonderful fairground ride in the world, until it was cursed by an evil wizard. Now all the people inside have been turned into goblins! "We may look a little weird, but we're not creatures to be feared."

Before they go any farther, the children will need some supplies! Each box contains an object that does not appear in the other box. Which two objects are they?

Help from you I now beseech. Which items are unique to each?

MAP

Enter the Impossible Maze

Ruby and Ned take the two unique items from the boxes, and Garibaldi leads them to a row of doors. He tells them that one will allow them to continue their journey into the Impossible Maze. Which door should they take?

Open the second door that's to the right; Of the leftmost door that's in your sight.

Descend as clocks are known to do; A clockwise turn will work for you.

Which way do the hands on a clock turn?

Stairs

Using Garibaldi's clue, they open the correct door and walk through. Ruby and Ned then discover two staircases leading down into the maze. Which one should they take?

Shadows

They descend the staircase and enter a dimly lit room. The goblin tells them they will need one other vital piece of equipment.

What item should Ned and Ruby pick?

It's something that was in the equipment crate— Remember darkness will be your fate!

Powering Up

Ruby and Ned pick the flashlight, but it is missing batteries. It needs two batteries that add up to eleven volts in total. Can you work out which two batteries they should use?

Too Many Doors

They turn on the flashlight and finally light up the entire room. Wow! The room is full of doors—and lots of goblins! But which way to go? Their goblin guide gives them a clue:

Which door does not have a goblin pointing at it?

Don't Turn Right!

Behind the correct door, they find a strange room with a winding path across it. The goblin tells them that they must make their way along the path to the other side of the room, but they must not turn right. What path should they take?

Locked In!

They find their way into what appears to be a goblin treasure room. But as soon as they step in, the doors slam shut, trapping them on the inside and Garibaldi on the outside. Can you find a key somewhere in the room that they might be able to use to unlock the doors?

Through the Ducts

Ruby, Ned, and Mungo enter the hidden air ducts within the building. They need to find a route to another room. Can you help them find their way?

A Game of Gems

Ruby and Ned have discovered the spell name, but now they need to find out which magic ingredients they need. The list is in a book locked inside one of these chests. Star Sparkle tells them to open the chest of the highest value.

To the Basement

Star Sparkle whinnies with excitement. Ruby and Ned now have everything they need! She stomps her hooves on the floor, revealing a hidden opening that leads down a flight of stairs. Ruby, Ned, and Mungo need to go down the stairs, but not all of them can take their weight. Which ones should they step over?

You should only use the stairs with prime numbers or multiples of three on them.

Mixed-up Ingredients

Now that the magic machine is working, Ned and Ruby just need to put the spell ingredients into it and say the magic words! Can you find all the ingredients that were listed in the book in the unicorns' chest?

The Greatest Ride in the World

Ruby and Ned cast their magical spell, and in the blink of an eye they are standing back outside the fairground ride, now restored to its former glory. Look, Garibaldi is human again and wearing a proper uniform! There's just one message they spot that reminds them of their adventure.

TIP: Look at page 62!

Chapter 1

Page 6 The backward writing on the scroll reads: "There is a secret door hidden in the fireplace."

Page 7 The letters on the machine spell the word TRAPDOOR.

Page 8 (Top) The bug is an insect, as it has six legs and not eight. The children are safe to lift the trapdoor.

Page 8 (Bottom)

The correct cogs have a star and a cross on them.

Page 9 Ruby types "the password," looking at the small letters on the keypad. "8, 4, 3, 7, 2, 7, 7, 9, 6, 7, 3."

Page 10 All the numbers on the rocks are prime numbers, except for 15, which is a multiple of 3 and 5.

Page 11 The fastest route takes 7 seconds.

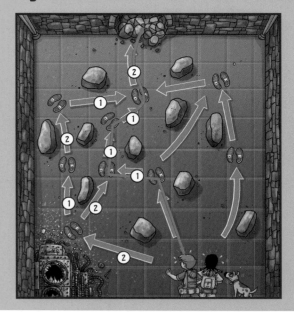

Page 12

Page 15

Page 13

Page 16 They should choose the fireplace marked 24, as that is a multiple of 3 and 8.

Page 17

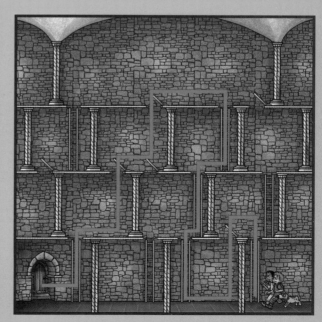

Page 14 The message reads:
"When fighting fire choose a multiple of both three and eight."

Page 18

Page 19

Page 20 (Top)

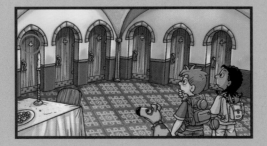

Page 20 (Bottom) Jack needs to serve bread.

Page 21 (Top)

Page 21 (Bottom) The items should be placed in the drawer in this order: knives, spoons, forks.

 **Page 22** The secret passageway is behind this picture.

 **Page 23** The knight's shield matches the shields of the knights on page 15.

Page 24

Page 25 there should be one of each symbol in each row and column. Press the buttons in this order:
1 = bird   2 = arrow
3 = star   4 = sword

Page 26 the children walked this way, and the castle was in the top right clearing.

Page 27 4 7 10 13 16 – each number is 3 higher than the one before.
27 22 17 12 7 – each number is 5 lower than the one before.
2 4 8 16 32 – each number is double the one before.
45 41 37 33 29 – each number is 4 lower than the one before.

Page 28

Page 29 there are nine knights hidden in the picture.

Page 30 Ruby and Ned can see Jack, the server they met.

Chapter 2

Page 32

Page 33 All of the animals on the signpost have left footprints. Here are some of them:

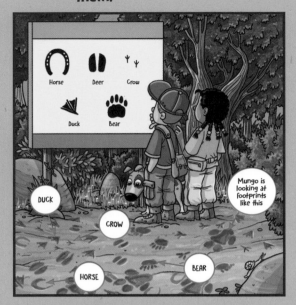

Page 34

Page 35

Page 36 They end up at G2.

Page 37 The creature is a dragon.

Page 38 (Top) The message says: "The flowers are magically heavy!"

Page 38 (Bottom) Remove the flowers in this order: orange, red, blue, yellow, purple, pink.

Page 39 The dragon says:
"I'm a garden dragon! I just love picking flowers, especially the tall ones. However, the pollen makes me sneeze, and dragon sneezes are magical!"

Page 40

Page 41

Page 42 Slide 18 goes to Gnome Town.
Slide 16 goes to Pixie City.
Slide 20 goes to Leprechaun Village.
Slide 49 goes to Dragon Town.

Page 43 The message reads:
MEET YOU IN THE TREASURE ROOM,
FRIENDS

Page 44 Ned and Ruby have not spotted that
their friend Snuffles is hiding with the
other dragons.

Page 46

Page 45

Page 47

Page 48 The correct map is this one:

B

Page 49 Snuffles can give all six flowers to
his dad. They all have five petals, and
6 flowers × 5 petals is 30, which is an
even number of petals.

Page 50

Page 51

Page 53 Pattern 2

Page 52

Page 54 Snuffles's gift to the children is a ruby ring.

Page 55

Page 56

Chapter 3

Page 58 The message on the wall says...

Please help us! Don't use the front door. Find another way in!

Page 59

Page 60

Page 61

Page 62 (top)

Page 62 (Bottom)
the secret message says:
THE GOBLINS ARE FRIENDLY.

Page 63 None of these keys will open the padlock.

Page 64 the code to open the padlock is 370.
Number of days in a leap year = 366
Number of keys on the keyring = 4
366 + 4 = 370.

Page 65

Page 66

Page 67

Page 68 (Top)

Page 68 (Bottom)

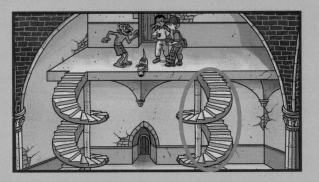

Page 69

Page 70 they need to pick the batteries marked 7V and 4V.

Page 71

Page 72

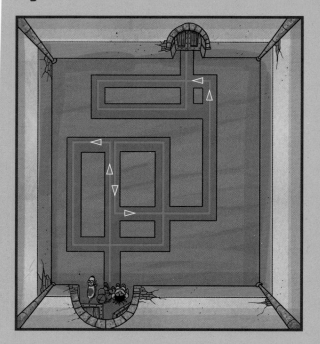

Page 74 They can use the air duct hidden behind the painting.

Page 73

Page 75

Page 76

Page 77 The name of the spell is Hocus Pocus.
There are seven stars on the unicorn's
back, which is an odd number.
The total number of points on the
stars is 7 x 5 = 35. That is not a
multiple of 6.

Page 78 The correct chest is A
A is 2 + 4 + 4 + 5 = 15
B is 2 + 2 + 3 + 4 = 11
C is 2 + 3 + 4 + 5 = 14
D is 2 + 3 + 4 + 5 = 14

Page 79 The children can use these steps.
2 = prime number
3 = prime number and multiple of 3
5 = prime number
6 = multiple of 3
7 = prime number
9 = multiple of 3
They should step over 1, 4, 8, and 10.

Page 80 The numbers that add up to 50 are
20, 18, and 12.

Page 81

Page 82 The sign reads:
THE RIDE IS OPEN